How To Win
At Ladies' Doubles

How To Win
At Ladies' Doubles

ALLEGRA CHARLES

ARCO PUBLISHING COMPANY
New York

Published by Arco Publishing Company, Inc.
219 Park Avenue South, New York, N. Y. 10003

Copyright © 1975 by Allegra Charles

Library of Congress Catalog Card Number 75-3780

ISBN 0-668-03797-0   (Library Edition)
ISBN 0-668-03794-6   (Paper Edition)

Printed in the United States of America

Contents

Foreword

Throughout my many years in tennis I have emphasized the importance of winning to my many students. It's the exhilaration of a win, and the anticipation of moving up a notch on the ladder, that makes tennis the addiction it becomes.

I started my tennis career by first taking group lessons as a child. My coach, or instructor as they are known in America, emphasized hard practice and physical conditioning. He also made it clear that as many tennis matches are won by the wits as by the racket. I spent years learning not only how to hit the ball, but also where to hit the ball. My years in tennis as a player and later as a coach have taught me that the major attraction of the game is that it is a never ending learning experience. I can still remember my winning points in major tournaments, and, probably more important, I can still recall my losing points in the big ones when I came in second.

Coaching tennis is a very rewarding experience. Players who have the natural ability or who start in the formative years only have to be led by the hand. The real challenge comes with the player who discovers the game as an adult. My book is written for her. It will show her basically how to think tennis. It will also bring out and develop her basic desire to win.

My job is to provide the know-how which will move the aspiring player up the ladder. Let's get along with it!

Introduction

I entitle this book *How to Win at Ladies' Doubles*. It is not a simple cookbook describing only the various grips and basic strokes. It will of course remind you to keep your eye on the ball and tell you when to take your racket back, but it will also tell you how to win at Ladies' Doubles, and how to move up the ladder at your club. It will describe and instruct you on how to play a game which differs, as you will see, from Men's Doubles.

The statistics I use so often in this book have been the result of keeping score and diagramming hundreds of ladies' doubles matches, and from them I have drawn the conclusions enclosed in these pages. It has been gratifying to instruct others using these guidelines, and to see that they work.

The first book written on the game of doubles in tennis was in 1956 by William Talbert and Bruce Old. There have been a number since, but they have all concentrated on Men's Doubles. To play championship Men's Doubles, it is essential to have an overhead which will produce a winner nine out of ten times. It is essential to be able to half-volley with effect, and to volley away most balls at shoulder height. Such shots are rare in Ladies' Doubles, and efforts on your part to execute them leave you with a high percentage of errors.

I will help you develop a winning game, a game you will feel comfortable with, and a thinking game. This game will not depend on shots that you have not yet developed.

The Psychology
of Winning

I'm sure that you have often heard the expression, "she's a winner." This usually refers in everyday life to the girl who seems to be able to accomplish with ease what others find almost too demanding to try. The "winner" appears to be at ease in difficult situations. The "winner" always has a little something extra to call on when needed. She is not easily flustered and her concentration is steady and sustained.

What I want you to realize is that you are not born a winner nor are you, to contradict a popular phrase, "a born loser." Winning is a learned behavioral response. Psychologically we learn habits and basically we all learn the same ones. What is then required is the appropriate motivation to enable us to use our habits to determine our behavior. It's that special motivation that carries the "winner" to the top.

In tennis the motivation to win comes quite easily because there is no gradation of performance; you either win or lose. First we have to learn how to recognize and deal with the critical points that win or lose matches. Once we have learned how to do this, we will, as a result, develop the confidence of a "winner." Successful performance will serve to further reinforce and expand our motivation.

Every time you go on the court you must have the feeling that you are there to learn; hence it's your obligation to yourself to leave the court with information that will make you a better player. This information can be negative as well as positive. If you lose match point, be sure to understand why. Was it your choice of shot? Was it that you were apprehensive?

Was it a beautiful shot by your opponent? Also think carefully about how you won match point and try it again in the same situation. Is it a successful pattern that will be part of your winning habit? Remember that ad in, game point, and set point are one and the same. These important points make you a winner or a loser. In developing habits you first have to make mistakes. The awareness of the mistakes will be the first step in eliminating them. This is rather easily demonstrated in tennis, but I'm always amazed at how often players make the same mistake time and time again. In the beginning it is unfortunately necessary to lose ten matches before you win one, but to look at this experience positively and to analyze what your opponents did to win and what you did to lose is what is so essential.

I'd like to give you a few specific hints that sometimes take years of play to come upon. I believe that these hints will call to your attention the fact that certain situations in a tennis match actually determine the outcome more than others. I have already mentioned that the ad points, game points, and set points are of utmost importance. Often forgotten is the importance of winning the third, or 40, point. Once you have reached this point, your opponents cannot afford to make an error or take a chance which is a decided factor in your favor. The single most important element in determining whether you win these very important points is for you to have a definite plan in mind. You should never allow the ball to play you. What I mean by this is that you should not react to where your opponents hit the ball; you should have a preconceived plan as to where you are going to hit the ball. This preconceived plan may be as simple as hitting to the backhand or forehand sides of the court or, in a singles game, even to the middle. The plan can be more specific such as employing a lob or drop shot. The point is that you know what you are going to do and your opponent doesn't. It doesn't make any difference whether the ball now comes to your forehand or backhand. You have programmed a plan and your body can react in a reflex way. The plan eliminates indecision and the split tenth-of-a-second it takes to react to your opponent's shot and plan yours. As you develop successful habits, you will learn which of your preplanned shots are the most successful in the important points, and you can call on them more frequently. In the meantime, the use of a preconceived plan will eliminate indecision and help you develop the confidence of a "winner."

Now why does this work? A tennis court is often "bigger than life." A specific portion of the court is a better target and easier to concentrate on. You can remember so many occasions when all you had to do to win the point was to hit the ball anywhere in the court because your opponent had either fallen or was drawn off the court by your previous shot. Of course, you missed it. If you had selected a specific spot to hit to, you would have easily made the shot. Another example of the value of picking a specific spot in which to place your shot before hitting the ball is seen in serving practice. Often I have asked an intermediate pupil to hit ten serves in. With the whole service court to aim at, five or six go in. When I place a can on the backhand side of the service court, the number of good serves improves dramatically. The same happens if I put the can at the center or on the forehand side. Planning the shot ahead and thus having a fixed mental target will help you to execute the shot properly.

The secret of how to win is to learn how to win. Know what points are important, preplan your shot, and, above all, be sure to understand why you lose when you do. You don't have to worry about the motivation to win. If you have made the effort to read this book, your motivation is obviously there. If you haven't yet developed winning habits, I assure you that it is not too late. Think tennis, observe, concentrate, and learn.

Ladies' Doubles –
How It Differs

There are many good books written on doubles, but they all describe what we see on the center court at Wimbledon. More specifically, they describe strokes, strategy, and play-making that apply to the very different game of Men's Doubles. We first have to recognize that we should put out of our heads thoughts, or rather dreams, of top-spin backhand winners, drop volleys, and half volleys. Important as they are to top flight men's tennis, they are statistically poor choices in the game we play. I emphasize the word "statistically," and I will come back to that word time and time again. Statistics is exactly what winning tennis is all about. You should always hit the shot that *statistically* has the best chance of crossing the net. I ask that you take a look at the following facts.

Fact 1

85 percent of points won in ladies' tennis are the result of your opponents' errors. I have scored hundreds of Ladies' Doubles matches, and have documented this amazing fact over and over again. This includes errors forced by your good shots.

Fact 2

15 percent of points won in a ladies' tennis match are the result of an outright winner. Already we see that since it is awfully difficult for us to increase our percentage of winners (e.g., more backhand zingers and aces), it makes much more sense to cut down our number of errors. Minimizing your errors is basically what I hope this book

will teach you. If I can get you positioned in the right place most of the time, and if I can get you to hit a shot that has a statistically good chance of crossing the net, you will win; I guarantee it. Now let me be more specific, and prove my point.

Proper Position

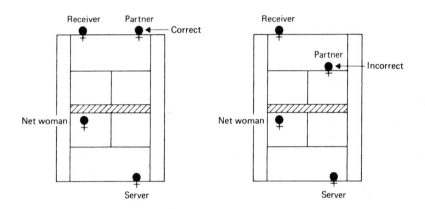

FIG. 1
Proper Position

If you are not familiar with the theory of both partners up together and back together, I will briefly explain it.

In doubles the basic strategy is to cause your opponents to have one person at the net and one person in the backcourt while you retain parallel alignment. This strategy allows you to hit a winner through the hole which results—that large empty space diagonally between your opponents (server and net woman, in Fig. 1). If you can get your opponents in this position, you can win the point 70 percent of the time. This statistic only applies if you and your partner are in a parallel alignment; either both at the net or both in the backcourt. Thus when serving, your job is to get to the net as soon as possible to join your partner. When you both are at the net and your opponents lob, you and your partner move to the backcourt together. The resultant parallel alignment eliminates the hole that exists when one player is up and one player is back. This strategy is so evident in Men's Doubles, but is so often forgotten in ladies' play.

How does the alignment strategy apply to returning serve? Tradition has placed the partner of the receiver at the service line, putting her in no-woman's land. She can be of little help to the receiver here, and can be compromised by balls hit to her shoe tops. She would be much less vulnerable if she would remain back, parallel to the receiver. Then, as the point progresses, hopefully with a good return of serve, the team is ready to attack the net together or stay back together as defenders. There is no hole through which the opponents can hit a winner.

The Important
Points

Certain points in tennis are of particular importance to win. We all know that psychology plays a role, and that teams lose matches they should have won because they were "uptight," "psyched," or just plain nervous. Again statistics can be helpful. The idea is to try to put your opponents into situations that will increase the mental stress upon them. We know that winning the first game gives you a headstart, and that teams winning the first game win the set 60 percent of the time. Likewise, winning the first point of a game awards you with a 60 percent chance of capturing the game. After winning the first set, try extra hard to win the first game of the second set. There is a tendency to let down a bit after winning the first set. The team that wins the first game of the second set after winning the first set wins the match 70 percent of the time.

Now let's consider the important points in a game. I've already mentioned the importance of the first point. The third point is a vital one to win. Once at 40, the pressure on your opponents is at its greatest. You have taken away their opportunity to try to hit a winner. They cannot afford an error now. This applies at 40-love, 40-15, or 40-30. Play conservatively, be sure to make no errors yourself, and let your opponents make the crucial error. Remember that 85 percent of points won result from your opponents' error. Concentrate on getting the first and the third points in each game.

Percentage Tennis

1. **Question**: When my two opponents are at the net, should I try to hit a shot to pass them?

   Answer: No; your chances of hitting a successful passing shot are small. Lob; there is less chance of making an error, and in addition it breaks up their formation.

2. **Question**: I am serving at 40–30. Shall I try to hit my serve a little harder to force an error on return or to ace my opponents?

   Answer: No; statistically there is little chance of aceing your opponents and a greater chance of faulting. Hit your usual three-quarter speed serve; the pace of your second serve should be the same as the pace of your first serve. The pressure is on your opponents, not you. If they make the error, you win the game.

3. **Question**: What do I do if I am passed down the alley while at the net?

   Answer: Utter, "nice shot!" Stay where you are, and hope that your opponents will try it again and again. Chances are that an opponent can pass you only two out of five times, so you will win the point three out of five times.

4. **Question:** What do I do when I'm out of position, or in doubt about what shot to hit?

   Answer: Lob. When in doubt, lob. It gives you and your partner time to get organized and back into the point.

5. **Question:** Should I play my opponent's weakness—usually her backhand?

   Answer: Don't count on it as you can in singles. Doubles play allows players to cover up backhand weaknesses. An opening is left when a player runs around her backhand, but her partner can usually cover.

6. **Question:** What should I practice?

   Answer: The serve, volley, drop shot, and lob. Your forehand and backhand ground strokes get enough practice, and you have devoted at least 75 percent of your court time to them already.

7. **Question:** What do I do with a deep high backhand?

   Answer: This is one of the hardest shots in tennis to return. Don't try to do anything fancy. Just get it back, preferably away from the net woman. A lob is your best bet.

8. **Question:** What do I do when I get to the net and am lobbed?

   Answer: a) If your partner is in the back court, she goes after it and you run to the area vacated by her to cover. (Refer to Fig. 2(a).)
   b) If your partner is also at the net, you have to go back for the lob. She also goes back on her side of the court so that you are now both in the backcourt. (See Fig. 2(b).)

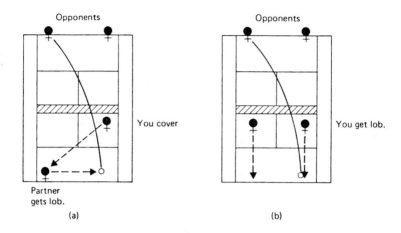

FIG. 2
Covering for the lob.

9. **Question:** Who should serve first on our team?

   Answer: The player with the best serve. Be sure that she also serves first in the second and third sets. At the beginning of each new set, either player may serve the first game.

10. **Question:** What points in a match are of increased psychological importance?

   Answer: a) The first point of each game.
   b) The third, or 40, point of each game.
   c) The first game of each set.

Partners

I think it best at first to play with as many partners as possible to observe various styles of play and to experience a bit of the give-and-take necessary to develop a good team. When selecting a permanent partner, it is most important for her to be a person you can communicate with freely. It is as necessary to discuss a match after it is over as it is to play it. Pick a partner whose game complements yours. This means that if you have a strong forehand, pick a partner with a strong backhand. If you both have poor overheads or both have weak backhands, it will be impossible to hide them from your opponents. Naturally one of you has to play the backhand court. My advice is to look for a left-hander. If you take your tennis as seriously as I do, be sure you pick a partner who wants to win. The longer you play together, the better you will become. You will learn to anticipate automatically where your partner will be in each situation. Being aware that she will take the lob over your head at the net will allow you to cover her vacated court. As you begin to think as a team, you will make it harder and harder for your opponents to find an uncovered area into which a winner can be hit. Remember that doubles is a thinking woman's game. The team that maintains the proper position (both up or both back) and forces their opponents into the one-up and one-back position will win the match.

Basics

Every tennis book must have a section devoted to basics. Basics must include a discussion of the various grips (the forehand, the backhand, and the serve), and we will cover this in detail in the next section.

At every level of tennis players will occasionally experience a slump. Opponents who usually offer no threat are now winning. Shots that routinely could be counted on are now inconsistent. The overall game that you worked so hard to develop seems to have left you. This is the time to go back to the basics. The answer to the problem is usually found when the basics are analyzed. A small change in grip or a different foot position while serving can drastically alter your entire game. This return to the basics is very important because the correction of the defect will emphasize to you just how vital the proper grips and strokes are. As your proficiency increases, the nuances of the various grips will become clearer to you. You can then experiment and experience, for example, a top-spin forehand using a western grip or even an American Twist serve. The advanced spin shots which offer variety and control to your game are possible only by a thorough understanding of the basic grips and strokes.

This book emphasizes strategy and will attempt to develop for you a thinking woman's game. You will find that you will be able to correct the flaws in your game by reviewing the basic section. It will be necessary to do this on numerous occasions, and from these repeated reviews will come the understanding fundamental to the development of a variety of shots. The combination of sound basics and an understanding of strategy will develop winning tennis.

60142

Grips

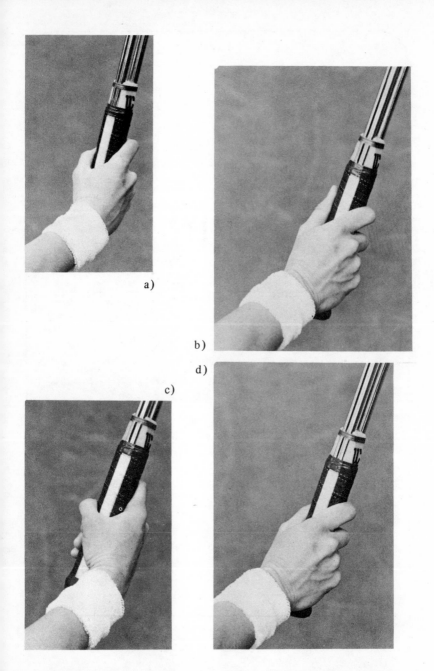

a) Eastern forehand, b) Continental forehand, c) Western forehand
d) Backhand

I will describe to you in detail the various grips, but I want to emphasize that if you are hitting the ball successfully with the present grip you are using, and by this I mean making good contact with the ball, then by all means stick with your present grip. This section will analyze the various grips and show that, whatever your grip, you can play successfully with it. After perfecting your strokes with your present grip, you may, after a thorough understanding, want to modify it or try others. Such experimentation should come only after you have fully developed the natural grip that you presently find comfortable. It is a definite mistake to start anew with a grip unfamiliar to you simply because your instructor teaches it that way.

For reference purposes when discussing grips, have your tennis racket in your hand, hold it straight out with the strings facing an imaginary net across the room. The top of the handle as you look down at it will be 12 o'clock and the bottom, underneath, will be 6 o'clock.

FOREHAND (right-handers)

1. Eastern

The V formed by your thumb and first finger is at the top of the racket at 12 o'clock. (See Fig. 3.) This is the most commonly taught grip, and will result in a forehand hit with little spin. It is referred to as a flat forehand. This grip is midway between the other grips and is the easiest to learn. Once learned, variations to the other grips are easier to appreciate. I

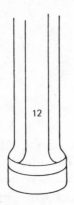

FIG. 3
The Eastern forehand grip.

suggest this grip to beginners, but do not change players who naturally use another grip.

2. Continental

The hand is turned counterclockwise around the handle until the thumb can be extended down the 9 o'clock handle position. (See Fig. 4.) This opens or tilts up the racket face. This is also the backhand grip. The open face imposes a slice or under spin to the shot which helps to hold the shot in, but at the expense of speed or pace. The Continental forehand grip was popularized by the famous Australian players after World War II. It is most effective when hitting a low bounding ball as seen when playing on grass. The present surfaces indoors and clay outdoors cause a higher bouncing ball which minimizes the effectiveness of the Continental forehand grip.

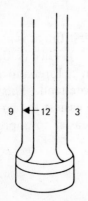

FIG. 4
The Continental forehand grip.

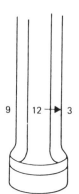

FIG. 5
The Western forehand grip.

3. Western

The hand is turned clockwise around the handle until the palm is at the 3 o'clock position. (See Fig. 5.) This is just the opposite of the Continental grip, and as a result closes or tilts downward the face of the racket. This grip imposes top spin or over spin on the ball. It is effective on high bounding balls commonly seen on hard surface courts. It is regaining popularity now that surfaces such as grass with its low bounce are being replaced by surfaces with a higher bounce. With this grip, the palm is at 3 o'clock. Remember that the backhand grip is at 9 o'clock so an extensive change must be made to hit a backhand.

FOREHAND (left-handers)

1. Eastern

The same. The V formed by the thumb and the first finger is at 12 o'clock. You are shaking hands with the racket.

2. Continental

The hand is moved clockwise to 3 o'clock; this is the same as the backhand grip.

3. Western

The hand is moved counterclockwise until the palm is at 9 o'clock.

BACKHAND (right-handers and left-handers)

Rotate the hand so that the thumb is extended down the back of the racket handle. This is the same as the Continental forehand grip for both right- and left-handers. To simplify changing to the backhand grip, remember always to cradle the throat of your racket with your other hand while waiting to hit a shot. This makes the grip change very easy. Once you have established this habit, grip change becomes automatic. An extension of cradling your racket with the other hand is to slide it to the handle and to hit a two-handed backhand. Small children who can't swing a racket with one hand, especially on the backhand, are often taught to use both hands. They sometimes carry this to perfection and stay with a two-handed backhand. Adults usually have the strength to hit a backhand with one arm. The disadvantage to the two-handed backhand is that your reach is shorter and as a result you have to run at least one more step to hit the ball.

SERVE

One sentence is all that is necessary to devote to the service grip. Use the Eastern forehand grip. What is ever so much more important is the proper toss of the ball. If the ball is not consistently thrown to the proper spot, you will not be able to make contact regardless of your grip. The Eastern forehand grip is the most comfortable and familiar. Concentrate on the toss and be sure to watch your racket meet the ball at impact. This will ensure a crisp hit.

The Forehand

Turn sideways and take the racket back as the ball crosses the net. Bend the knees, step forward into the oncoming ball, and watch the racket hit the ball.

The most common problem in tennis is hitting late. By this I mean that preparation to hit the ball is not made until the ball crosses the net. It is now too late for you to perform the three fundamental steps essential for hitting a good shot: to turn sideways to the net, to take your racket back, to step forward and hit the ball. If you turn sideways, you can hit the ball simply by swinging your arm forward toward the net, which is the direction your shoulder is constructed to move. If you step forward, you shift 120 pounds into the ball at impact which eliminates the need to swing very hard. A gentle stroke with the weight moving forwards allows you to contact the oncoming ball in the center of the racket in contrast to a hard swing which makes good contact difficult. Take your racket back as you step sideways. Don't exaggerate this motion. It only makes you late in hitting. A big loop or exaggerated backswing is unnecessary. Your shot is determined at impact and your backswing is only to get your racket in a position to hit the ball. A short backswing and a step into the oncoming ball is all that is required. Naturally you can't step into the ball if you are standing at the spot where the ball hits the court. Always stay at least one step behind the baseline. It is easier to run forward than backward, and by moving in for the ball you can be sure your weight is going forward during the hit. You will find it difficult to stand this far back in the beginning, but force yourself to do it. Soon you will see that you can run up to get most short balls. By remaining a step behind the baseline, you will always be able to step forward to hit balls that are hit deep to you. If you stand on or inside the baseline you will be forced to hit deep shots off your back foot as you move backwards to get the ball. These difficult shots always result in a weak return if you are able to get them back at all.

Those fundamentals eliminate late hitting. Hitting the ball in front of you is only possible if you step forward. You can step forward only if you play back; again, one step behind the baseline. Take your racket back early as you turn sideways, and after a short backswing, hit the ball as your weight moves into it. Another common fault is getting too close to the ball as you hit it. Your best shots will be hit when you reach for the ball with your arm extended. Staying one step back from the baseline ensures this. Constantly go over these fundamentals. They will produce the proper forehand stroke.

The Backhand

a)

b)

c)

a) Turn sideways and take racket
back while dropping front shoulder.
b) Step forward and hit. c) Finish
follow-through with racket high.

Let me begin by saying that the backhand stroke, contrary to what you think, is the easier stroke to hit. The only reason it seems harder is that you have hit five times as many forehands as backhands in your lifetime of tennis and, as a result, your forehand is more comfortable and accomplished. To begin a rally, you drop the ball and hit a forehand over the net to your opponent. Think of the thousands of times you have done this and you will see how much more practice your forehand has received. Stop that immediately. Drop the ball and hit it backhand to begin your rallies. When you are standing sideways to the net, your arm is in front when hitting a backhand and this is an advantage. You can hit the ball in front of you by simply swinging at it as you step forward. When hitting a forehand, your arm is behind the rest of your body and has a longer way to go to hit the ball in front of you. It's going to take time to develop your backhand so favor it all you can. It will help to play the backhand court in doubles, and as mentioned before, hit a backhand when you drop the ball to start a rally. When you gain confidence in your backhand and can use it as an attacking, forceful stroke, your game is on the way to rapid improvement. Favoring your forehand will hold you back forever.

As with the forehand, you have to take your racket back as you turn sideways. Your weight should shift forward as you step into the ball. Again, playing one step back from the baseline will ensure this weight shift when stepping forward to hit. Another important factor is to have your knees bent, rather than rigid, while hitting. If your knees are rigid and you bend at the waist to reach and hit the ball, you will hit down and cause the ball to go into the net. By bending your knees, you are on the same level as the ball and your stroke will carry the ball up and over the net. Positioning yourself sideways to the net and stepping forward to hit automatically puts you in this knees-bent position. Remember to cradle your racket with your other hand. This allows you to change easily to the backhand grip with the thumb down the back of the racket. Most players have neglected their backhand, and have never experienced the exhilaration of fully hitting a crisp crosscourt backhand with their body weight going forward. Keep at it until you hit just one correctly. You will know instinctively when you've executed a good backhand, and from then on you will see that the backhand is the more natural and satisfying ground stroke.

The Serve

a)

b)

c)

d)

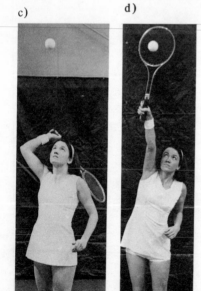

a) The ready position. Pause here. b) The proper throw of the ball is essential. The elbow is extended and the palm is up. c) Hit the ball at the top of the throw. d) Watch the ball as you hit it to ensure solid contact.

The most important shot in tennis is the serve. By throwing the ball up and hitting it at your opponent you have an advantage that you don't lose until she actually executes a return. She hasn't a hint of the serve's pace, its spin, or its placement, whether to her backhand or forehand, until it cross the net. Her lack of anticipation creates a decided advantage for you. If her return is poorly hit you have a partner at the net to hit the winner for you which is another advantage peculiar only to the server.

Statistically, the server wins the point 65 percent of the time, the receiver, 35 percent of the time. Thus you can recognize how important it is not to double fault. I suggest that you hit a three-quarter speed serve both times. This means that you don't try to hit a hard first serve and a soft second serve. With the statistical edge in your favor, you really can't afford not to take advantage of it. If you hit the same three-quarter speed serve for both the first and second serve, you will increase your ability to get it in because of the additional practice. Practically speaking, there are very few aces hit in a three-set Ladies' Double match. Remember, get the serve in and you will most likely win the point. I find that the easiest serve to get in is a slice serve which will cross the net high and drop into the service court. A flat serve has a tendency to carry long since it has no spin to hold the ball in. Practice!—take a little off your first serve and hit two of them. It won't be long before you will notice the improvement.

Inconsistency in throwing the ball up to the same place each time is the most common cause for poor serving in tennis.

This is to be expected since you have to throw the ball with your wrong hand. The secret is to extend your arm palm-up, and throw the ball without bending your elbow. If you bend your elbow, the ball can go anywhere. Extend your arm until you feel tightness at the elbow, and throw the ball up a little in front of you. Once you can rely on the ball being in the same place each time, serving will become much easier.

Another common fault is not watching the ball as you hit it. If you watch the racket hit the ball, you can be sure of good contact. The ball will then be hit in the center of the strings rather than off the frame or peripheral strings. This simple hint is invaluable in developing consistency in your serve. Remember that although the windup and the proper follow-through do help your serve, hitting the ball in the center of your strings at impact is really what determines its effect.

It is usually best to try to serve to your opponent's backhand. Before you try to place your serve, be sure you can get that three-quarter speed serve in one out of every two times. Until you have achieved this consistency, just hit your serve and don't worry about its placement. Avoid double faulting. It is too hard in this game to win a point. Don't give any away.

Return of Serve

The second most important shot in tennis is the return of serve. You hit a return of serve exactly as many times as you hit a first serve. It pays to devote some time to learning to return serve. As previously mentioned, you are at a statistical disadvantage in returning serve. Sixty-five percent of the time you will lose this point. What can we do to improve this statistic? First of all, as soon as we hit the ball back over the net, the statistic changes, and now we have a 50 percent chance of winning the point. We have managed to take away the server's advantage by just getting the ball back over the net. That's quite a reward considering that our return was nothing fancy. It would be nice if you could drive a low forehand or backhand to the ankles of the onrushing server, but consider the great incidence of error of such a shot. Don't forget the advantage the server has by throwing up a ball and pounding it down at you. Just get it back, that's all you have to do. I certainly don't mean for you to hit a cripple to the net woman, but you have the option of hitting the ball anywhere on the server's side of the court or lobbing over the net woman.

A word about returning the second serve: Never try to hit the second serve back for a winner. We all do this, and it is one of the biggest mistakes made in ladies' tennis. The server who faults her first serve is apprehensive, and the advantage is now swinging your way. Her next serve will certainly be easier to return, and to get it back across the net, which is your objective, should be no trouble for you. Don't try to overhit and negate the opportunity to have a 50 percent chance of winning the point. Repeat this to yourself as you await that second serve.

A common mistake in returning serve is to watch the server instead of the ball while your opponent is serving. Watch the ball as it is thrown and watch it as she hits it. This will give you an additional tenth of a second to ready your return. Watching the loops and eccentricities of the server doesn't give you enough time to find the ball in flight and prepare your return. This small bit of advice is one of the most helpful hints I can offer you.

The Lob

One of the most underrated shots in tennis is the lob. The lob can open up wonderful opportunities for you. It can drive the net woman back, and if her partner doesn't follow her, your opponents will have left the diagonal hole open. The lob can also get you out of the most drastic situations. When in doubt, lob. How many of your friends can hit an overhead winner from behind the service line? One of the hardest shots in tennis, isn't it? You can also use the lob for an occasional service return. The lob has a high percentage of success of going in. This accomplishes just what you want with a return of service.

Lobs should be high. It is also nice to get them deep, but just high will do. When high, they give you time to scurry to your proper position, and, in addition, a high lob gives your opponents more time to worry about their overheads. Forget the top spin lob; it goes too low and is unpredictable except when Rod Laver hits it. Remember to practice a few lobs when warming up. When your opponents want overhead practice, this is the time to concentrate and perfect your lob. The lob is a lethal weapon in Ladies' Doubles and should be used often.

The Overhead

a)

b)

a) Carefully watch the ball and get ready.
b) Turn sideways and take the rocket back.
c) Watch your racket hit the ball. This ensures solid contact.

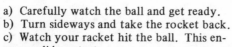

c)

Throughout this book I have emphasized the lob as an extremely important shot in Ladies' Doubles. If your opponents have read this book, you had better know how to hit an overhead. An overhead! Does the sound of that frighten you? Well, it needn't. This shot's complexity is overstated by most books on tennis. The overhead is hit exactly the same way as the serve, except that you can hit it anywhere on the court rather than having to hit it into the service square. (See Fig. 6.)

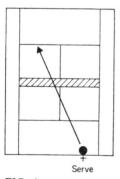
Serve

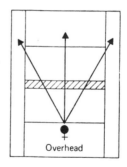
Overhead

FIG. 6
Placement of the overhead.

In Ladies' Doubles, placement of the overhead is helpful, but more often than not just hitting the ball in the court with the pace of a serve is good enough to win the point. The difficulty lies in judging the fall of the ball. It is harder to hit a falling lob than a ball tossed in the air for serving. You must practice the technique and, until you have adequate experience, let all lobs bounce and hit them exactly as you do the serve.

This eliminates the only difficult part of hitting an overhead. Make sure to get back quickly enough and far enough. Think of it as a serve rather than an overhead. Hit your usual three-quarter speed serve. Don't try to baby it or place it. The overhead requires the same free-swinging motion as the serve. It is essential that you watch your racket hit the ball to ensure good contact and a crisp hit.

The Volley

Upper) The forehand volley. Step forward, watch the ball, meet it
with a short jab. Lower) The backhand volley. Turn sideways,
bend the knees, watch the ball, and just meet it with the racket.

There is only one reason to be at the net and that is to score. You have one shot at the ball and you have to make it a winner. You are not there to hit the ball back to your opponents, you are there to win the point. The best way to do this is to hit the ball off the court as quickly as possible. In other words, you must hit the ball diagonally so that it bounces to the outside of the court. Hitting it deep is most likely hitting to where your opponents are, and the longer flight of the ball gives your opponents more time to catch up to it. Hit a short diagonal shot. (See Fig. 7.) It doesn't have to be too hard. This will be the shortest route to a winner.

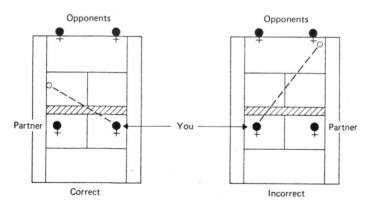

FIG. 7
Placement of the volley.

A volley should not be stroked like a backhand or forehand ground stroke. It should be punched. You don't have time at the net to take your racket back and then step forward.

You should step toward the oncoming ball while simultaneously sticking out your racket; then you need only to let the force of the oncoming ball supply the power to your shot. It's really very easy this way because all you have to do is meet the ball. Even with this short jab, you can get great power. Most ladies, unfortunately, step back from the oncoming ball, but this habit can be easily corrected once you get the sweet feel of your weight going forward and cracking a volley that you have simply met with your racket. Remember, don't hit it back to your opponents; hit it diagonally away from them.

Poaching

I've already mentioned that you are at the net for only one reason and that is to score. So often a team gets into trouble by an incorrect approach to poaching. As net woman, you have the option of crossing to your partner's side to hit a volley. You must in your own mind consider the shot as a set-up which you feel you can volley away for a winner. This is the rationale for a poach. Once started, don't change your mind. You are now committed to carry on. If you miss the shot or can't get to it, your only hope is a gracious apology to your partner. After her attempt the poacher should then remain on the side to which she has crossed.

When your partner poaches and you are in the backcourt, what do you do? This is a very important consideration. We don't want both players, one behind the other, on the same side

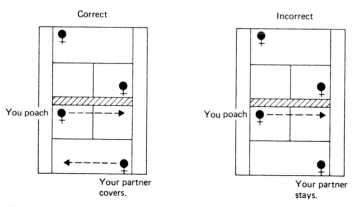

FIG. 8
The poach.

of the court. Therefore your job is to run immediately to the opposite backcourt, which results in your partner being at the net on one side and you in the backcourt on the other. (See Fig. 8.) You hope your partner's poach volley will result in a winner, but if it doesn't, expect a lob return, and you will be in position to get to it.

Poaching is effective on occasion, and is useful in breaking the pattern of a successful crosscourt service return. Don't do it too often. *Never* roam back and forth at the net because your partner will not know where to cover. Remember that the ideal formation is both players up at the net and that is what you are trying to achieve.

The Drop Shot

I've always been surprised that this important shot is used so little in ladies' tennis. Show me a team with a drop shot, a good lob, and a consistent three-quarter speed serve and I'll show you a winner.

A drop shot is a ball that is hit with little pace. The idea is to hit the ball only a short distance beyond the net. The drop shot is used when your opponents are deep in the backcourt. It forces your opponents to make a long run, and, what is even more important, once they get to the ball (close to the net), they have a difficult return shot to execute. (Refer to Fig. 9.) If your opponents do happen to return the drop shot, you now have them in that one-up, and one-back position so advantageous to you.

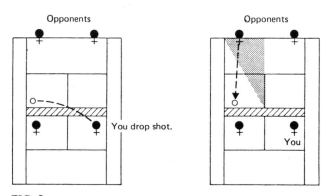

FIG. 9
The drop shot.

To hit a soft ball a short distance over the net encompasses two principles. First, the ball should be hit with slice, which means under spin. Secondly, the ball should be hit with your weight going backward, or at least not going forward. This weight displacement isn't too hard once we consider that most of our poorly hit ground strokes are the result of not shifting our weight forward. Just let instinct take over; don't step forward; then slice. The slice allows you to carry the ball on your racket longer, thus enabling you to guide the ball to the desired spot.

Practice your drop shots with your partner on the other side of the net in the forecourt hitting drop shots back. This can be a great deal of fun for both of you. Proficiency comes quickly because, again, this is a rather natural shot.

I will now tell you what to do when you are the receiver of a drop shot. There are two choices. The first choice is to hit to a drop shot back and the second is to lob. The lob is difficult because you are close to the net and have only half the court length to lob into. It is also difficult to lob when running forward.

How to Get
to the Net

Getting to the net is often easier said than done. The rule is that you come to the net on all balls hit short by your opponents. Ideally you should also come to the net behind your serve. When your partner is at the net, your every thought should be to join her as soon as possible. With both partners at the net, you have statistically a better chance to win the point than your opponents. Coming to the net on a short ball hit by your opponents is easy. You have to run up to hit the shot and you just keep going to the net. The important thing to remember is that your partner should join you at the net. Coming to the net behind your serve is more difficult. There are two options here. You can hit the return of serve as a volley on your way in, or you can await the return of serve in the backcourt. If you choose the latter, you must return the ball diagonally to the opponent in the backcourt or lob over the opponent near the net. The lob is often easier for it gives you more time to get to the net. Whichever choice you make, be decisive. Don't hesitate or stop or you will be caught in no-woman's land, halfway up and halfway back from the net.

Once at the net, you and your partner apply a great deal of pressure on your opponents. You have everything covered except the alleys, and more losers than winners are made hitting for the alleys. There is also a tendency for a player to watch the person at the net rather than the ball. This always results in an error. The psychological pressure put on your opponents by you and your partner being at the net often wins unexpected points for you.

Review
of the New
Alignment
for
Ladies' Doubles

The best strategy in Ladies' Doubles is to have both players parallel on the court, either both up at the net or both in the backcourt. Statistically, you have the best chance of winning any specific point if you are in this alignment. Conversely, you should try to maneuver your opponents into a one-up and one-back alignment to create a diagonal opening through which to hit a winner.

We all begin doubles matches, when receiving, in a traditional one-up and one-back configuration. This should apply only to top-flight Men's Doubles. Men of any lesser ability get into trouble because they are caught one-up and one-back with the nearest to the net watching rather than helping, and a backcourt player unable to get up. This very problem is also the problem in Ladies' Doubles. Figure 10 illustrates the change I propose and have found to be successful.

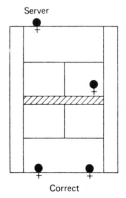
Correct

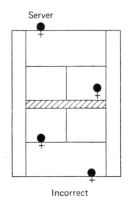
Incorrect

FIG. 10
Position when receiving serve.

When your team is receiving, it is best to have both players in the backcourt. This alignment will eliminate the diagonal hole in your formation which a poaching net woman is looking for. You and your partner should both play back while you are at the decided disadvantage of receiving the serve. Remember the server has a 65 percent chance of winning the point, and you must get back to a 50-50 situation by returning the serve. Another reason to eliminate the traditional placement of a player at the service line, halfway up, is that any ball hit to her has to be returned by a volley from her shoe tops or a half volley. These are difficult and defensive shots and very seldom win points. It is much better to be back together and then to go to the net together on a short ball or a lob which drives your opponents back. Naturally, when serving, your partner is at net and it is to your advantage to join her. You can follow your serve in, hoping for a high, soft return to volley, or you can await the return in the backcourt and go to the net with your next deep, ground stroke. All of these alignment considerations are presented graphically in Figs. 11 through 19.

FIG. 11
The conventional doubles alignment to receive serve. Note the vulnerable position of the receiver's partner. She is forced to hit a low volley or a half volley.

FIG. 12

The preferred doubles alignment to receive serve. The receiver's partner is back. From this position she can return any shot with a ground stroke or a lob.

FIG. 13

The net player volleys to the feet of the opponent who is in the vulnerable midcourt position.

FIG. 14
The net player volleys through the diagonal hole produced by the opponents' one-up, one-back alignment.

FIG. 15
The net players' volleys can be easily returned when both receivers are back. A passing shot or a lob is in order.

FIG. 16
When the net players are lobbed, they both move back together. Both being at the net together or back together eliminates the diagonal opening created by the one-up, one-back alignment.

FIG. 17
Both players are back after being lobbed. The court is covered.

FIG. 18
With the server back, the net woman is lobbed.

FIG. 19
The server crosses to take the lob and the net woman crosses at the net to cover. The server should come to the net to join her partner after lobbing or after the opponents have hit her a short ball.

Gameswomanship

SPINNING YOUR RACKET FOR SERVE
AT THE BEGINNING OF A MATCH

If you win the toss, you have the option of picking the side of the court on which you want to play the first game or the choice of serving or receiving. Think about this again. You can choose:

1. to serve
2. to receive
3. to play on either side of the net

The factors to take into consideration are:

1. Have you had time enough to warm up your serve? Remember how important the first game is. If you are not warmed up neither are they, and it might be an advantage to receive.
2. Consider the sun and the wind. You always want your stronger server serving into the wind.
3. Psychology: If you choose to receive or to take the opposite court, you will confuse your opponents. They now unexpectedly have to serve across the net from where they warmed up.

Once you have made your choice, your opponent can select from the remaining options. If you choose to serve, your opponent has choice of court. If you choose the court, your opponent decides whether to serve or receive.

Have your choice prepared prior to the spin of the racket. Pick smooth. It seems few people do, and it sets you apart from the average "rough" team. Make a point of being serious about the racket toss. You know it's not that important, but your opponents don't.

IN OR OUT

The U.S.L.T.A. rules state that the decision as to whether a ball is in or out is made by the player on the opposite side of the net from the player who hits the ball.

In Ladies' Doubles the problem usually arises on the return of serve. The job of the receiver of the serve is to return the serve. The job of the receiver's partner is to call the serve out if it's out. The receiver often returns a questionable ball, but a brisk call of "out" from her partner stops play. How many times have you played a serve that was out, or made a poor return of serve when in doubt about whether the serve was good? When receiving, return the serve and let your partner make the call.

ORDER OF SERVICE

At the beginning of each set, a team may decide which partner serves first. The order may be changed at the beginning of the next set if so desired. This rule gives you the opportunity of starting each set with your big server.

A DISABLED PLAYER

The U.S.L.T.A. regulation states that if a player is unable to continue to play on account of physical unfitness or an unavoidable accident not within her control, she must be defaulted. I know you wouldn't make use of this rule, but if your dastardly opponents do, you will at least know that they are legally correct.

THE NET

Make a point of checking the net prior to the beginning of the warm-up period. Actually, this is quite important because the net is invariably high. Never have I known it to be low. One racket down and one sideways equals the three-foot center height. Always ask the opponents to help. They now know you mean business even before you hit a ball. Keep them guessing.

Conditioning
and
Practice

Most of today's women tennis players have taken up the game rather recently. Some had early tennis experience at camp during childhood, but most did not begin to play seriously until recently. A good number of men are playing tennis seriously for the first time too, but they have a definite advantage, which accounts for the initial rapidity of their progress. First, it has always been traditional for most American boys to learn to throw baseballs and footballs as they grow up, but it was unusual for a girl to be taught to throw a ball twenty years ago. The tennis serving motion is identical to the arm motion used in throwing, and, therefore, most men are familiar with this fundamental movement. The serve is the single most important shot in tennis and it is necessary to practice faithfully until consistency develops. Not many of you have your own tennis court, and renting court time at your indoor club to practice serving is rather extravagant. If you can find a court available and have the time, serving fifty balls a week will be extremely helpful. I feel that at least a thousand serves are necessary before you develop the proper consistency and placement. As an alternative, it is extremely helpful to practice throwing a tennis ball with the overhand motion of a baseball player. Certainly this is second best to actual serving practice, but the development of the proper serving motion can be hastened considerably by this exercise in throwing. The driveway is an ideal spot and the garage door can be the target. Fifty throws a day will do wonders for your serve.

Tennis is a game of quick starts and stops, long runs, and endurance. Until recently, girls in America were not brought up to do such things. Boys, during their baseball, basketball, and football years, acquired such abilities early and have since found it rather easy to apply these valuable habits to tennis. What is so remarkable about the world's best tennis players is not only their superb shots, but also their unbelievable ability to run and change directions. If filmed in slow motion, their movements are as graceful and exact as those seen in a ballet.

Tennis is a game of running. If you can run down every shot, your opponent cannot score. To do this, first you have to know how to run, and second, you have to have endurance. Knowing how to run sounds rather basic, but after watching women run day after day, I've come to the conclusion that they are inexperienced. Actually this inexperience shouldn't surprise you, for, very few girls, as kids, were expected or taught to run, and later it was thought to be unladylike to sweat. You had better get over those notions quickly. In winning tennis you have to be prepared to work.

Walking up and down stairs, carrying groceries, and scrubbing floors doesn't develop endurance. I propose that you run a mile every day, unless you play tennis that day. This isn't as difficult as it sounds. Running a mile takes about ten minutes of your day. You can do it after the children go off to school or after dinner at night. These are the times when it is least likely that you will meet the people who will inevitably ask what you are doing. After a month of running you will find that you have a noticeable increase in your endurance. You will never tire in the third set and you will never have the heavy legged feeling. What's more important, you will, for the first time in your life, be learning to run efficiently. By running I mean what is commonly referred to as jogging in America. You should run at your own pace. It is not the speed that you are after, but the leg conditioning. A mile course can be easily mapped out using your automobile speedometer, and can be conveniently located with your home or children's school at the end point. I emphasize the importance of running because I feel that it is so critical and so easy to practice.

Now that you have mastered the throwing motion that is so important in the development of your serve and you have been running a mile a day guaranteeing endurance in the third set, what more must you do in regard to practice? First of all, recognize the fact that your ground strokes will get enough practice over the years during the games, sets, and matches you play. While warming up, prior to a match, be sure to practice your volley and overhead. These shots are difficult to practice at any other time and are essential shots in a doubles match. Ground strokes, backhand and forehand, can be best practiced off a backboard. Backboard exercises take patience because they can become very tiresome. Remember the fact that a half hour spent on the backboard is equivalent to a month of play mainly because you hit so many balls during backboard practice.

A relatively new innovation is the ball machine, which can be extremely valuable if used properly. I don't feel that the ball machine can be of much help with ground strokes because you don't have to run and change position to hit the ball. The ball is hit directly at you which is quite different from what you experience in a match. The ball machine, however, can be of value in volleying and can be set up to offer you overhead experience, both of which are difficult to practice any other way.

This book emphasizes that winning tennis is something that is learned. Familiarity with proper strokes and their execution are important, but strategy and a knowledge of the game are equally important. Play as much as you can. Analyze your wins and defeats and learn from your mistakes. The more you play, the better your strokes will automatically become. What you have to do, in addition, is to be aware of the fact that most points in tennis are won as a result of your opponents' errors. It follows that it is your obligation to keep the ball in play as long as you possibly can. To do this, it is obviously essential for you to develop physical endurance.

Concentration

Concentration is essential to playing your best tennis. Concentration can be defined as the ability of the player to be totally concerned about the specific point she is playing. She is simultaneously aware of the score, aware of her opponents' weaknesses, and aware of her own plan for her next shot. These thoughts are all-consuming and exclude distracting influences such as crowd noise, court conditions, and weather. The secret is to concentrate on each individual point, not on the set or the match in general. This way you have one specific goal to attain: to win that point. It is much easier to maintain concentration if you consider each point individually.

The most common cause for reduced concentration is temperament. No one likes to lose a tennis match, but it is very important that we learn how to handle losing. Tennis is such a fast game that you can't ever brood over losing an individual point. If you do, your concentration is interrupted and the level of your play will suffer in successive points. Forget quickly the point you just lost and readjust your thinking to plan for the next point. Once a point is over, it should be totally dismissed from your mind. Game temperament is something that is learned. No one is born who isn't nervous and somewhat apprehensive on the tennis court. What you have to do to overcome this is to learn to concentrate on nothing else but the point you are playing at the moment. Don't let your opponents' idiosyncrasies, net cords, or court manners affect you. Also don't let errors that go against you—your double fault or missed overhead—affect your concentration. Think of the next point. Your attitude carries across the net and can affect the confidence of your opponent. If your opponent senses that your concentration is broken by a show of temper, she knows that he can usually count on the next few points. Don't be led into a casualness on the court especially if you are playing someone whom you consider to be a weaker player. Casualness, like a show of temper, breaks your concentration and causes your game to suffer.

Good court manners go hand in hand with concentration. Attention to the point being played will eliminate indecision and mistakes in the score. So often such incidents upset your pattern of point concentration. Recognize the fact that your opponents will hit some nice shots. Don't let their good performance upset you, and what's more, don't be overly complimentary since this boosts your opponents' confidence. Your opponents are as nervous as you are, and you have no obligation to encourage them. Acknowledge a good shot, but be ready to win the next one. Don't let your emotions show. Keep your opponents unaware of your tensions and be oblivious to theirs.

The above aspects of temperament can be learned and are not uncontrollably a part of you. Again, the easiest way to remain calm, and thus maintain concentration, is to think only about the point being played. Dismiss the last point from your mind. If you do this, you will conceal your nervousness and emotions from your opponent. The point being played is enough to demand your complete attention.

The Tie Breaker: 5 Out of 9 Points

1. The tie breaker is played when the score reaches 6-all in any set.
2. The player whose turn it is to serve, serves points 1 and 2 from the court he usually serves from. The server next in rotation on the opposing team serves points 3 and 4. The original server's partner then serves points 5 and 6. The second server's partner follows by serving points 7 and 8, and 9 if necessary. Each player serves from his established side, changing courts when it is necessary to do so to serve from the usual side. Point 9 is served from the right or left court at the election of the receiver.
3. After the tie breaker, the next set is begun by having the second server of the tie breaker begin serving from her customary side.
4. Strategy in a tie breaker is quite different from regular game strategy. Each point is crucial: much more so than in a regular game. You can't afford a foolish error. You can't afford to take a high risk shot. Your shots must have a high percentage of success and a low margin of error. Thus it is essential that you get your serve in; remember that the server wins the point 65 percent of the time and the receiver 35 percent of the time. Don't try for an ace. The pressure is on the receiver. Don't try flashy passing shots. Try high percentage lobs. Force errors from your opponents. Above all, be aware of the score and call it out. Concentrate on making very few errors by always hitting the safe shot. By winning the fourth point, you increase the pressure on your opponents. It is now vital to maintain

your parallel alignment, either both up or both back. You can now wait for the opportunity to hit a sure winner, or continue to hit safe shots until the pressure of the situation combined with your alignment causes your opponents to make an error.

Tennis Rackets

I have very strong feelings about the selection of a tennis racket. It is extremely important that your racket not be too heavy nor have a grip that is either too large or small.

The most common mistake made in tennis by players of all levels is to be late in hitting the ball. We all are guilty of watching the ball cross the net and then taking our racket back to prepare our shot. By then the best you can do is hit the ball alongside of you. What you always want, and should do, is to hit the ball in front of you as you step into it. To make up for this late hitting you should use the lightest racket possible. You will be able to get a light racket around faster, thus minimizing the effect of hitting late.

The metal racket with the open throat has been a "godsend" for late hitters. It's not that metal rackets are lighter, for they come in various weights as do wooden rackets, but the open throat eliminates the wind resistance encountered during the swing. This reduction of wind resistance allows the racket to come around faster, and allows you to hit the ball in front of you. The open throat is also an advantage in serving. Good serving requires the server to be able to snap her cocked wrist just prior to hitting the ball. This action speeds up the racket considerably at the time of impact and produces the speed on the serve. The same is true in golf. The snap of the wrists at the time of impact is what accounts for the distance of the drive. The server who hits with a perfectly straight arm and no wrist action can never achieve pace and spin. The open throat racket, again by reducing wind resistance, allows you to get that something-extra into the serve. If, by the simple choice of a racket, you can improve the most important stroke in the game, your serve, and make up for the most common mistake in the game, late hitting, you had better buy a metal open throat racket.

There are certain advantages, or to be more accurate, preferences, to wooden rackets. Being more flexible, they hold the ball on the strings longer to give you that certain feel of the ball and, along with it, a bit more accuracy on ground strokes. The metal rackets, being stiffer, cause the ball to fly off the strings faster, resulting in greater speed but less feel or accuracy. In my opinion, the advantages of the metal open throat racket far outweigh the disadvantages.

The average woman's grip size is 4½. If you get a grip too large, you will be unable to hold onto and control the racket. If your grip is too small, you will develop hand cramps from gripping too hard. A size 7 glove takes a 4½ grip.

A light racket is easier to swing, offers an advantage in serving, and helps to eliminate late hitting. Rackets are usually marked according to grip size and weight. I advise a 4½, light.

There has been much written about racket strings as to type and tightness. It all sounds so very complicated but actually it is very simple. Strings are of two types, gut and synthetic, the most popular synthetic being nylon. Gut strings are rougher and thus abraid or scratch into the surface of the ball, holding the ball on the surface of the strings longer. This extended contact allows you to place the ball more accurately. I define this control factor as "feel." Along with the advantage offered by control is the disadvantage that gut strings are extremely variable in their tensile strength and break more easily. They are also affected by temperature and humidity. You can count on them breaking after you return from two weeks at the seashore. Nylon strings are slippery and thus the ball tends to slide off the strings, resulting in less control. The main advantage is that nylon lasts much longer than gut and is unaffected by changes in humidity and weather.

A common misconception is that the tighter you string your racket, 60 pounds or over, the harder you will hit the ball.

A tightly strung racket plays like a wooden paddle. You don't get the trampoline effect that increases the speed of the ball. In addition, the ball leaves the racket face so quickly that you also get very little feel. A racket strung at 50 pounds allows the ball to indent the strings and the result is speed and accuracy. The longer the ball is on the racket face the more opportunity you have to control its placement.

My suggestion then is to use a light, metal, open throat racket strung at 50 pounds with nylon. You will be able to get wrist action in your serve and hold the ball on your racket long enough to achieve good feel and accuracy.

Court Surfaces

Indoor (carpets, rubber mats)

These surfaces are the slow ones which most of us play on during the winter. The ball bounces high and is hard to hit away for a winner. Scramble on this surface and run down everything. You will be surprised how many balls you can get back. Your opponents will occasionally reward you by missing an easy shot. Since it is very difficult to hit a winner (ace, volley) on such a surface, most points are long and won when an error is made. Drop shots are very effective.

Clay

This surface is similar to the indoor surface but produces a little skid on the bounce. It is a slow surface productive of long rallies. Again, run for everything. Don't try for aces. Drop shots are ideal. You will be surprised how many points will be won by just getting the ball back.

Hard surfaces (macadem, concrete, fast drying hard surfaces)

Play is faster here. Aces and winners are easier to hit and more frequent. You should volley more, and hit fewer ground strokes. Drop shots aren't as effective. It is even more important on this surface for your team to be both up and back together to eliminate open areas for your opponents' volleys.

Tennis Elbow

This condition seems to affect more women than men. I believe that this is due to the fact that the sudden popularity of tennis among women has put a racket in the hands of many ladies who haven't experienced such stress exerted on their elbows before. In contrast most men have been swinging bats and clubs throughout their formative years, thus protecting their elbows by muscular conditioning.

The classic tennis elbow results in soreness at the outer aspect of the elbow, and is caused by the tearing and secondary inflammation of the muscle tendons as they attach to the bone at the elbow. It is caused by overextending your elbow and having it extended even farther as the force of the ball strikes your racket. This overextension happens every time you hit a backhand, particularly if you don't hit it squarely. If you have doubts about whether you have a tennis elbow or not, just extend your arm to put a quart of milk into the refrigerator. If you experience pain at the outer aspect of the elbow, you have tennis elbow. Other elbow ailments such as pain at the inner side of the elbow usually subside with heat, rest, and time.

The only therapy that I have found of benefit in acute tennis elbow is a cortisone shot. Often this has to be repeated to get the cortisone to the exact spot, but it is universally successful. A forearm brace helps to bolster the elbow against the force of the ball hitting the racket with an extended arm and can be beneficial; however it will not cure tennis elbow. Just plain rest helps the pain, but doesn't move you up the ladder, and the pain will return with the first backhand you hit improperly. A light wooden or open throat metal racket will allow you to bring the racket around faster, thus eliminating late hitting which overstresses the elbow. Hitting the ball in front of you with your weight going forward puts much less stress on your elbow. Hitting late makes it necessary for your arm to supply all the power in the shot, and thus strains your elbow.

Tennis and Sex

Much has been written regarding the level of athletic performance and how it can vary with the same individual at different times. We all have good days and bad days. The effect of sexual intercourse prior to an athletic event, as a rule, is to cause a decrease in the level of performance. Naturally, this can vary from individual to individual, but overall concentration and performance suffer. I'm at a loss to explain the physiological basis of this fact, but there appears to be a time period necessary to restore the body to its prime athletic performance level. This time span for me is six to twelve hours and appears to be rather uniform in female athletes. I feel that each woman has her own individual pattern, but, as with the menses, we react collectively much the same.

We are all aware of the effect of the menses on our own daily performance, mental attitude, and our athletic functioning. There is no doubt that tennis is more difficult to play at that time of the month. I have tried to convince myself that it is just my mental attitude, but I have no doubt that my performance level is lowered. I suggest that, whenever possible, you eliminate your voluntary ladder matches during the menses. Naturally you should play if challenged, but don't voluntarily present a challenge during this time.

The effect of tennis on pregnancy is certainly more beneficial than harmful. There is no reason for you to stop or limit your play during the first six months of an uncomplicated pregnancy. The exercise will help to keep you from gaining unnecessary weight, it will be beneficial to your mental attitude, and you will observe that there is no decrease in your performance level. After the sixth month, I feel that you can certainly rally for exercise, but I would suggest that you don't play competitively until after delivery. Often after delivery there is a desperate desire to get back to the courts. I feel that your doctor should make the decision as to when you can resume play. Usually, play can be begun one month after delivery.

Quiz

1. You are serving and your partner is at the net. What should be your plan?

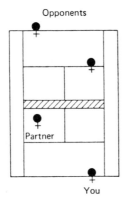

Opponents

Partner

You

FIG. 20

Right	Wrong	
		1. I should either volley the return of the serve to the back opponent on my way to the net or stay back and stroke the return of serve to the back opponent. Next, I should go to the net to join my partner as soon as I can force a short return.
		2. Stay back on the return of serve and trade ground strokes with the back opponent.
		3. Try to ace the receiver.
√		*Answer* 1. Your job is to join your partner at the net as soon as it is feasible, either by a first volley or

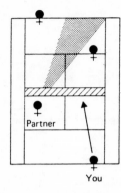

FIG. 21

Right	Wrong
	√
	√

by way of a follow-up ground stroke. At the net your partner has an opportunity to volley any ball hit to her into the shaded diagonal (see Fig. 21). When you get to the net, your opponents will be in the one-up, one-back situation.

2. Staying back and trading ground strokes with the back opponent leaves you in the up-back situation vulnerable to a poach.

3. An ace is a poor percentage shot in Ladies' Doubles.

2. I am receiving serve and my partner is at the service line in the traditional alignment. What should I do to win this point more often?

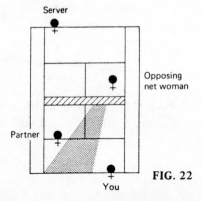

FIG. 22

Right	Wrong	
		1. I should change the alignment, and send my partner to the backcourt.
		2. I should try to pass the net player.
		3. I should hit a good return applying pressure to the onrushing server.

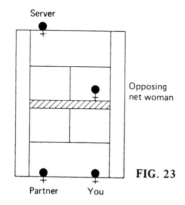

FIG. 23

Answer

Right	Wrong	
√		1. Your partner should move to the backcourt. You are now in a parallel position leaving no openings. All you have to do is get the ball back to the server, and you have an equal chance to win the point. This strategy is very successful in Ladies' Doubles.
√		2. Trying to pass the net player would force you to hit a shot that has a low percentage of success.
√		3. A paced return of service is difficult. The server has a decided advantage when she throws a ball up and pounds it at you. Your job is to get it back in any way possible, and to play the point from there. If you are able to do this, you have a 50 percent chance of winning the point.

3. We are both in the suggested back position awaiting serve. What should we do with the serve?

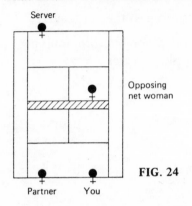

FIG. 24

Right	Wrong	
		1. Return it to the server trying to keep her back.
		2. Lob over the net woman.
		3. Return the serve as above, and go to the net together on a short return to us or after we lob.

Answer

The alignment of both partners back allows a number of options and relatively safe shots. Most important, it removes your partner from a position in which she must hit a difficult volley or not participate in the point.

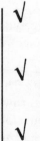

√		1. First you have to get the serve back. Don't be too fancy with your return; just get it back and eliminate the server's initial advantage.
√		2. A lob over the net woman is a good shot on occasion, especially if the server always comes to the net on her serve.
√		3. Your job, and your partner's, is to get to the net together. This can be done when your opponents hit a short ball or when you "lob them back". Remember when you and your

| **Right** | **Wrong** | partner are at the net together you have the best percentage statistically of winning the point. |

4. My partner and I are together at the net. Where do we hit the winning volley?

1. Through the short diagonal.

2. Down the middle deep.

3. To the deep corners of the backcourt.

Answer

Volley into the shaded areas shown in Fig. 25.

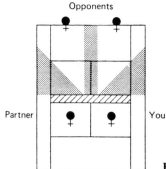

FIG. 25

1. If both opponents are back, volley to the shaded short diagonal areas. It will give your opponents the longest run. The volley doesn't have to be hit hard. If the opponent does get it, she is now up at the net and her partner is in the backcourt leaving a diagonal opening for you to exploit with your next shot.

2. Your second choice is to volley down the middle. This causes confusion and hesitation among all but the best teams. A return passing

Right	Wrong

shot from here is almost impossible. The volley should be crisp and deep into this area. Be alert for a lob return.

√ (Wrong) 3. Don't volley to the deep corners of the backcourt. Your opponents are there and will return the volley. Remember you volley to hit a winner.

5. My partner and I both have weak volleys. What strategy should we use?

1. Learn to volley.

2. Employ the usual alignment.

3. Lob a lot.

Answer

√ 1. Rely on your strength, which is your backcourt game. You will eventually begin to learn to volley, but on the Ladies' B and C ladders, teams can play winning tennis from the backcourt.

√ 2. First of all, the strategy must be reversed. Instead of striving to get both players up to the net together, you must strive to remain in the backcourt together. (Fig. 26) Remember never one up and one back.

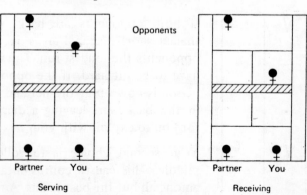

FIG. 26

Opponents

Partner   You
Serving

Partner   You
Receiving

Right	Wrong
√	

3. You had both better have an awfully good lob, because you will have to use it often to keep your opponents away from the net. Catch them up and back and use your ground strokes to hit the ball through the open diagonal. Scramble for every point, and always hit the safe shot. Again, emphasize the lob.

6. What should I look for in a permanent partner?

1. The best girl player in the club.

2. A player with a game similar to mine, but with strengths to complement my weaknesses.

3. A player new to the game with a big serve and great potential.

4. My best friend whose game equals mine.

5. A take-charge girl who plays well.

Answer

√

1. The best girl player will complement your game as a good partner should, but if her ability is greater than yours, she will frequently go for shots out of her territory thus getting the team out of position. Your opponents will play to the weaker member of the team.

√

2. It is best to have a partner with equal ability, but with a game that is strong in your weaker areas and vice versa. If your forehand is better than your backhand, find a partner with a backhand better than her forehand or find a left-hander. Her volley may be better than her ground strokes, which will be a help if you are strong on ground strokes and weak on the

Right	Wrong	
		volley. Play some singles with her. If the games are close, she will be a good partner.
	√	3. Not a winning team. Remember that winning tennis is thinking tennis. A player new to the game has too much to think about and strategy is often forgotten.
	√	4. This is a tough one. A good team must be able to communicate freely. They must be able to criticize and accept criticism. Many teams break up. Do you want to take the chance of losing your best friend?
	√	5. One husband is enough.

7.   Do you know your statistics?

1. You have a better chance to win a game when your team is serving.

2. Certain points in tennis are more important than others.

3. I have a better chance of not double faulting if I hit a hard first serve and then a soft one.

4. A good forehand drive is the same whether it is hit crosscourt or down the line.

5. Tie breakers are fair to all.

Answer

Right	Wrong	
√		1. You have a 65 percent chance of winning the game if your team is serving.
√		2. The first point is important psychologically. Winning the third point, thus achieving 40-0, 40-15, or 40-30, puts tremendous pressure

Right	Wrong	

on your opponents. They can't afford an error physically or mentally.

√ (Wrong) 3. Not for long. By hitting a three-quarter pace first serve two times, you will soon perfect your serve to the point that you rarely double fault.

√ (Wrong) 4. The net over the alley is four or five inches higher than at the center court. Down-the-line shots have a lower percentage of success.

√ (Wrong) 5. The strong server has a distinct advantage in the tie breaker.

8. What do we do when it is evident that our opponents are a superior team?

1. Look for their weaknesses and exploit them.

2. Increase the pace of our shots.

3. Play our own game.

4. Think tennis.

5. Consider it a rewarding experience.

Answer

√ (Wrong) 1. They are well aware of their weaknesses and have the ability to cover them.

√ (Wrong) 2. Certainly not. Never try to hit with a big hitter.

√ (Right) 3. Absolutely. It's what brought you to where you are. You are familiar with your game, but your opponents are not.

√ (Right) 4. Most important. Your shots may not be as good but your brain is. A sound understanding of the game will pull many an

Right	Wrong
√	

underdog through. Remember where you should be on the court and be there. Make them hit winners and hopefully errors.

5. A good loss teaches you a lot more than an easy win.

9.   How does Ladies' Doubles differ from Men's Doubles?

1. There should be a different alignment in receiving serve.

2. Fewer aces are hit.

3. Fewer half volleys and shoe-top volleys have to be hit.

4. More lobbing is essential.

5. Strategy is more important than power.

Answer

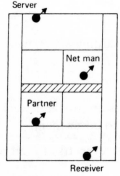

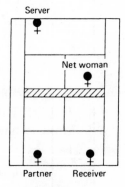

FIG. 27

Men's Doubles   Ladies' Doubles

1. The difference in Ladies' Doubles is that the receiver's partner is in the backcourt. (Fig. 27) Being back together is an advantage. The court is well covered, and the receiver's

Right	Wrong	
		partner is now less restricted, and can be of more help to her partner.
√		2. The serve should be reliable and hit deep. Attempts to hit aces usually result in double faults.
√		3. Moving the receiver's partner back from the traditional one-up, one-back position accomplishes this. The one-up, one-back position forces shoe-top volleys and half volleys to be hit because the up player is not close enough to the net to hit a proper volley.
√		4. The employment of more lobbing in Ladies' Doubles provides a good reason for improving both your lob and overhead.
√		5. Having the court covered and forcing your opponents out of position will win the point. Placement of shots is necessary, not power.

10. What shots are most important for a winning Ladies' Doubles Team and in what order?

Order	
	Reliable serve
	Strong backhand
	Strong forehand
	Lob
	Overhead
	Drop shot
	Return of serve
	Volley

Answer

Order	
1.	A reliable *serve* means hitting two three-quarter speed serves that you can count on, not a hard first serve and a soft second serve.
2.	The *return of serve* is the second most important shot in tennis. It need be nothing fancy; just get it back.
3.	The *volley* is the point getter. Don't swing; reach out and punch the ball in front of you.
4.	The *lob* is of next importance in Ladies' Doubles; hit it high and deep.
5.	The *overhead* is important to return the many lobs you are going to face. An overhead is hit just like a serve only it is easier to get in. Let it bounce, if necessary, and then hit it.
6.	The *drop shot* is a sure winner in ladies' tennis. It is easy to hit, and also fun to practice.
7.	At least one partner should have a *strong backhand*, but it is not essential that both partners have one.
8.	One *strong forehand* per team will suffice.

Glossary
and
Bibliography

Ace A serve that the receiver is unable to touch with his racket.

Ad An abbreviation for advantage. The next point after deuce. Ad-in means your ad and ad-out means your opponents' ad.

Alley The added width necessary for a doubles court. A doubles court is 4½ feet wider on each side.

Approach shot The shot hit prior to advancing to the net.

Backcourt The area of the court nearest the baseline.

Backhand The stroke hit from the left side of the body by a right-handed player.

Baseline The back boundary line. You serve from here.

"Baseline game" Forehands and backhands from the backcourt with little or no net play.

"Big game" The game characterized by a hard serve, a move up to the net, and the execution of a volley.

Bye An automatic win which advances a player to the next match in a tournament.

Cannonball A flat, hard serve hit without spin or slice.

Consolation tournament A separate tournament for those who lose their first match in the regular tournament.

Crosscourt A shot hit in a diagonal direction.

Default To concede a tennis match because of injury or other inability to play.

Deuce A tie score after 40-30, 30-40 or an ad.

Double fault The loss of the point after failing to get either of two serves in.

Doubles A game in which two players are matched against two opponents.

Down-the-line A shot hit straight ahead toward the sideline of the court.

Drive A ball hit hard without spin.

Drop shot A soft shot hit just over the net.

Error To fail to hit the ball over the net or within the opponents' court.

Fault   Failure to get a serve in the service court.

Foot fault   The server's foot steps on or over the baseline prior to hitting the ball.

Forced error   A shot hit so well that the opponents' return is weak and misdirected.

Forehand   The stroke from the right side of the body by a right-handed player.

Forecourt   The area of the court from the service line to the net.

Game   The point after 40, or ad-in, or ad-out.

Ground stroke   A forehand or a backhand stroke hit after the ball bounces.

Half volley   Hitting the ball on a short hop just after it bounces.

Ladder   Players listed according to their ability.

Let   A serve that touches the net before going in the service court. It must be replayed.

Lob   A high, looping shot usually hit over the head of a net player.

Love   Zero in scoring.

Match   A contest usually won by the player or players who win two sets. Some championship matches are 3 out of 5 sets.

Match point   If you win this point, you win the match.

Net game   Volleying at the net.

Net cord   A volley or ground stroke that hits the top of the net and goes in.

No-woman's land   The area of the court near the service line. It is difficult to volley or hit a ground stroke from here.

Overhead   A high ball hit with a serving motion.

Pace   The speed of the ball.

Passing shot   A ball hit straight ahead to either side of the opponent which he cannot reach to return.

Poach   To cut off and hit a ball at the net by crossing over to your partner's side of the court in doubles.

Point   A unit of scoring. The first point scored is called 5 or 15 and the last is called game.

Placement A planned shot hit far enough away from the opponent that it cannot be returned.

Rally An exchange of shots all hit after the bounces.

Receiver The player who returns serve.

Round Robin A tournament in which every player plays a determined number of games against every other player.

Seeding Ranking of players in a tournament to ensure that those with a higher ranking don't play each other in the first round of the matches.

Service A serve.

Service break The server loses the game.

Set A contest in which the first player or players to win 6 games, or two games in a row if tied at 5 games each, wins.

Set point The next point wins the set.

Singles One player matched against another.

Slice A ball hit with a slanted racket creating back spin.

Sidelines The left- and right-court boundary lines.

Top spin A ball hit with a forward over spin in contrast to a back spin or slice.

Toss To throw up the ball to serve.

Volley To hit the ball in the air before it bounces.

Addie, Pauline Betz, *Tennis for Everyone*. Washington: Acropolis Books, 1973.

Barnaby, John M., *Racket Work; the Key to Tennis*. Boston: Allyn and Bacon, 1969.

Bradlee, Dick, *Instant Tennis; a New Approach Based on the Coordination, Rhythm and Timing of Champions*. New York: Devin-Adain Co., 1962.

Brent, R.S., *Pattern Play Tennis*. Garden City, N.Y.: Doubleday, 1974.

Budge, Lloyd, *Tennis Made Easy*. New York: Ronald Press, 1945.

Connolly, Maureen, *Power Tennis*. New York: Barnes, 1954.

Cooke, Sarah, *Winning Tennis and How to Play It*. Garden City, N.Y.: Doubleday, 1946.

Cutler, Merritt Dana, *The Tennis Book*. New York: McGraw-Hill, 1967.

Danzig, Allison, *The Fireside Book of Tennis*. New York: Simon and Schuster, 1972.

Davidson, Owen, *Great Women Tennis Players*. London: Pelham Books, 1971.

Driver, Helen, *Tennis for Teachers*. Madison, Wis.: Monona-Driver, 1964.

Faulkner, Edwin J., *Tennis: How to Play It, How to Teach It*. New York: Dial Press, 1970.

Forte, Vincent, *Why You Lose at Tennis*. New York: Barnes & Noble Books, 1973.

Gallway, W.T., *The Inner Game Of Tennis*. New York: Random House, 1974.

Gonzales, Pancho, and Hawk, Dick, *Tennis*. New York: Fleet Publishing Corporation, 1962.

Graebner, Clark, *Mixed Doubles Tennis*. New York: McGraw-Hill, 1973.

Hart, Doris, *Tennis With Hart*. Philadelphia: Lippincott, 1955.

Higdon, Hal, *Champions of the Tennis Court*. Englewood Cliffs, N.J.: Prentice-Hall, 1971.

Hopman, Harry, *Better Tennis for Boys and Girls*. New York: Dodd, Mead, 1972.

King, Billie Jean, *Billie Jean*. New York: Harper and Row, 1974.

King, Billie Jean, *Tennis to Win*. New York: Harper and Row, 1970.

Lardner, Rex, *The Complete Beginner's Guide to Tennis.* Garden City, N.Y.: Doubleday, 1967.

Lardner, Rex, *The Underhanded Serve: Or How to Play Dirty Tennis.* New York: Hawthorn Books, 1968.

Laver, Rodney, *The Education of a Tennis Player.* New York: Simon and Schuster, 1971.

Laver, Rodney, and Collins, Bud, *Rod Laver's Tennis Digest.* Chicago: Follett Publishing Co., 1973.

Leighton, H.C., *Junior Tennis.* New York: Sterling Publishing Co. 1962.

Lichtenstein, Grace, *A Long Way, Baby.* New York: William Morrow and Co., 1974.

Metzler, Paul, *Getting Started in Tennis.* New York: Sterling Publishing Co., 1972.

Mottram, Tony, *Play Better Tennis.* New York: Arco Publishing Co., 1971.

Murphy, William, *Tennis for Beginners.* New York: Ronald Press, 1958.

Pearce, Wayne, *Tennis.* Englewood Cliffs, N.J.: Prentice-Hall, 1971.

Ramo, Simon, *Extraordinary Tennis for the Ordinary Player.* New York: Crown, 1970.

Richards, Gilbert, *Tennis for Travelers.* Cincinnati: Richards Industries, Inc., 1972.

Riggs, Robert, *Court Hustler.* Philadelphia: Lippincott, 1973.

Robinson, Louie, *Arthur Ashe: Tennis Champion.* Garden City, N.Y.: Doubleday, 1967.

Scott, Eugene, *Tennis: Game of Motion.* New York: Crown, 1973.

Seewagen, George L. and Sullivan, George, *Tennis.* Chicago: Follett, 1968.

Talbert, William F., *The Game of Doubles in Tennis.* New York: Holt, 1956.

Talbert, William F., *The Game of Singles in Tennis.* New York: Lippincott, 1962.

Talbert, William F., *Bill Talbert's Weekend Tennis.* Garden City, N.Y.: Doubleday, 1970.

Tilden, William T., *Match Play and the Spin of the Ball.* New York: American Lawn Tennis, 1925.

Trabert, Tony, *Winning Tactics for Weekend Tennis*. New York: Holt, Rinehart, and Winston, 1972.

Trengove, Alan, *How to Play Tennis the Professional Way*. New York: Simon and Schuster, 1964.

United States Lawn Tennis Association, *Official Encyclopedia of Tennis*. New York: Harper and Row, 1972.

Wills, Helen, *Tennis*. New York, London: Charles Scribner's Sons, 1928.